My State INDIANA

By Christina Earley

TABLE OF CONTENTS

A Crabtree Seedlings Book

Crabtree Publishing
crabtreebooks.com

School-to-Home Support for Caregivers and Teachers

This book helps children grow by letting them practice reading. Here are a few guiding questions to help the reader build his or her comprehension skills. Possible answers appear in red.

Before Reading:

- What do I know about Indiana?
    - *I know that Indiana is a state.*
    - *I know that Indiana has some good sports teams.*
- What do I want to learn about Indiana?
    - *I want to learn which famous people were born in Indiana.*
    - *I want to learn what the state flag looks like.*

During Reading:

- What have I learned so far?
    - *I have learned that Indianapolis is the state capital of Indiana.*
    - *I have learned that more than 200 species of animals live in Indiana Dunes National Park.*
- I wonder why...
    - *I wonder why the state flower is the peony.*
    - *I wonder why the first capital of Indiana was Corydon.*

After Reading:

- What did I learn about Indiana?
    - *I have learned that Indianapolis is the largest city in Indiana.*
    - *I have learned that the state bird is the cardinal.*
- Read the book again and look for the glossary words.
    - *I see the word **capital** on page 4, and the word **torch** on page 12. The other glossary words are found on pages 22 and 23.*

INDIANA

I live in Corydon. My town was the first **capital** of Indiana!

Many people visit Corydon to see the Indiana **Caverns**.

Indiana is in the midwestern United States. The capital is Indianapolis.

Fun Fact: Indianapolis is the largest city in Indiana.

The state bird is the cardinal.

The **peony** is the state flower.

We grow a lot of corn. Some of it is used to make corn muffins.

Fun Fact: Indiana is one of the states that grows the most corn in the U.S.

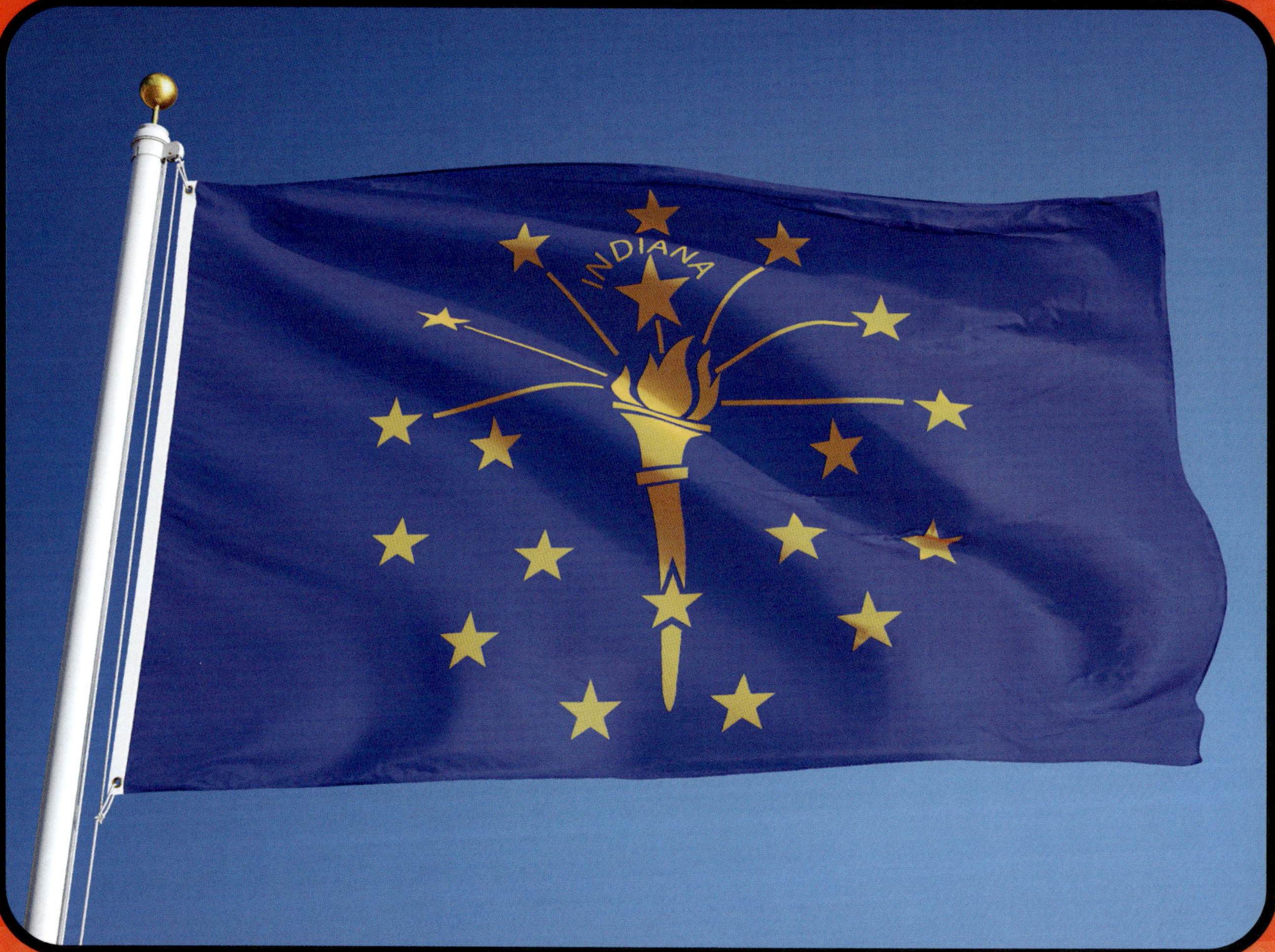

My state flag is blue. It has a golden **torch** in the middle.

There are two national sports teams in Indiana.

I like to visit Indiana **Dunes** National Park. I look for different birds and animals.

Fun Fact: More than 200 kinds of animals live in the national park.

I love going to football games at Notre Dame Stadium.

I enjoy boating on Monroe Lake.

Singer Michael Jackson was born in Indiana. NBA **legend** Larry Bird was also born in Indiana.

Fun Fact: Pete Buttigieg, the U.S. Secretary of Transportation, was born in South Bend, Indiana.

I like to take pictures at The Children's Museum of Indianapolis.

I have fun with my family at Indiana Beach amusement park.

Glossary

capital (cap-ih-tuhl): The city or town where the government of a country, state, or province is located

caverns (kav-ernz): Large caves, usually underground

dunes (dewnz): Hills of sand formed by the wind

legend (leh-jind): A very famous person who is known for doing something well

peony (pee·o·nee): A type of plant with large pink, red, or white flowers

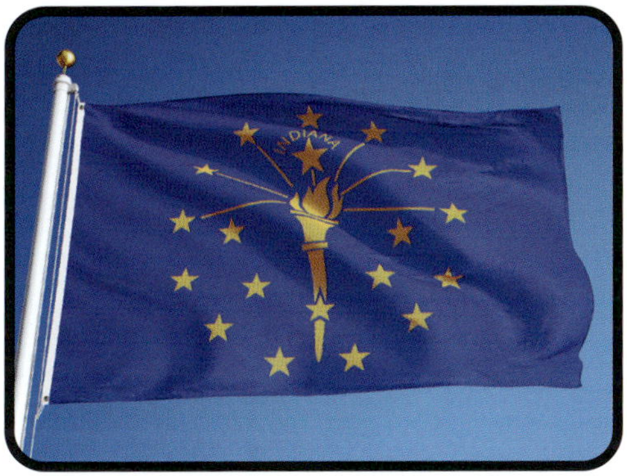

torch (tawrch): A long stick with burning material at one end

Index

About the Author

Christina Earley lives in sunny South Florida with her husband and son. She enjoys traveling around the United States and learning about different historical places. Her hobbies include hiking, yoga, and baking.

Written by: Christina Earley
Designed and Illustrated by: Bobbie Houser
Series Development: James Earley
Proofreader: Melissa Boyce
Educational Consultant: Marie Lemke M.Ed.

Photographs:
Alamy: Mindy Fawver: p. 4, 22; Don Smetzer: p. 17; MARKA: p. 18 right, 23; David R. Frazier Photolibrary, Inc.: p. 20
Shutterstock: Patricia Elaine Thomas: cover; Grindstone Media Group: p. 3; Garrett Wolf Hoffmaster: p. 5, 22; Volina: p. 6; Sean Pavone: p. 7; Jeff Caverly: p. 8; Serhii Brovko: p. 9, 23; Serg64: p. 10-11; Africa Studio: p. 11; railway fx: p. 12, 23; Jamie Lamor Thompson: p. 13; Delmas Lehman: p. 14-15, 22; GARRETTGCRAIG: p. 15; HunterMatthew: p. 16; landmarkmedia: p. 18 left; Andrew Cline: p. 19; Elizabeth C. Zurek: p. 21

Crabtree Publishing

crabtreebooks.com 800-387-7650

Printed in the U.S.A./012023/CG20220815

Published in Canada
Crabtree Publishing
616 Welland Avenue
St. Catharines, Ontario
L2M 5V6

Published in the United States
Crabtree Publishing
347 Fifth Avenue
Suite 1402-145
New York, New York, 10016

Library and Archives Canada Cataloguing in Publication
Available at Library and Archives Canada

Library of Congress Cataloging-in-Publication Data
Available at the Library of Congress

Hardcover: 978-1-0398-0247-6
Paperback: 978-1-0398-0257-5
Ebook (pdf): 978-1-0398-0277-3
Epub: 978-1-0398-0267-4

INDIANA

Welcome to Indiana! Come with me, Harlow, as I show you around the state where I live. Learn about my state's flag, bird, and flower. Find out my favorite activities too!

Books In This Series Include:

Alabama
Alaska
Arizona
Arkansas
California
Colorado
Connecticut
Delaware
Florida
Georgia
Hawaii
Idaho
Illinois
Indiana
Iowa
Kansas
Kentucky
Louisiana
Maine
Maryland
Massachusetts
Michigan
Minnesota
Mississippi
Missouri
Montana
Nebraska
Nevada
New Hampshire
New Jersey
New Mexico
New York
North Carolina
North Dakota
Ohio
Oklahoma
Oregon
Pennsylvania
Rhode Island
South Carolina
South Dakota
Tennessee
Texas
Utah
Vermont
Virginia
Washington
West Virginia
Wisconsin
Wyoming

Teacher's Guides

Crabtree Publishing
crabtreebooks.com

GRL: M
ISBN 978-1-0398-0257-5
90000
9 781039 802575